Touching
in Living Things

Karen Hartley, Chris Macro, and Philip Taylor

Heinemann Library
Chicago, Illinois

©2000 Reed Educational & Professional Publishing
Published by Heinemann Library,
an imprint of Reed Educational & Professional Publishing,
100 N. LaSalle, Suite 1010
Chicago, IL 60602
Customer Service 888-454-2279

Designed by Celia Floyd
Illustrated by Alan Fraser
Originated by Ambassador Litho
Printed in Hong Kong / China

04 03 02 01 00
10 9 8 7 6 5 4 3 2 1

Library of Congress Cataloging-in-Publication Data
Hartley, Karen, 1949-
        Touching in living things / Karen Hartley, Chris Macro, and Philip Taylor.
             p. cm. — (Senses)
        Includes bibliographical references and index.
        Summary: Describes how the sense of touch works in humans and animals and how they use it.
        ISBN 1-57572-251-8 (lib. bdg.)
        1. Touch Juvenile literature. [1. Touch. 2. Senses and sensation.] I. Macro, Chris, 1940-   . II. Taylor, Philip, 1949-
. III. Title. IV. Series: Hartley, Karen, 1949-   Senses.
QP451.H16 2000
573.8'75—dc21   99-38260
                                                                                        CIP

Acknowledgments

The Publishers would like to thank the following for permission to reproduce photographs:

Corbis/The Purcell Team, p. 10; Evans International/Greg Balfour, p. 26; Heather Angel, p. 23; Heinemann/Gareth Boden, pp. 4, 5, 6, 8, 11, 13, 15, 24, 25, 27; Image Bank/L. D. Gordon, p. 7; Oxford Scientific Films, p. 20, Oxford Scientific Films/Hans Reinhard, p. 22; Oxford Scientific Films/Martin Dohrn, p. 29, Oxford Scientific Films/Martyn Colbeck, p. 16; Oxford Scientific Films/Sean Morris, p. 28, Oxford Scientific Films/Stan Osolonski, p. 19; Pictor International, p. 17; Planet Earth Pictures/Joyce Photographics, p. 18; Tony Stone/Chip Henderson, p. 12, Tony Stone/Jess Stock, p. 14; Tony Stone/Lori Adamski Peek, p. 21.

Cover photograph reproduced with permission of Oxford Scientific Films and Gareth Boden.

Some words are shown in bold, **like this**. You can find out what they mean by looking in the glossary.

CONTENTS

WHAT ARE YOUR SENSES?

Senses tell people and animals about the world around them. You use your senses to feel, see, hear, taste, and smell. Your senses make you feel good and warn you of danger.

Senses are important to you and other animals. This book is about the sense of touch. You will find out how touch works and what you use it for.

WHAT DO YOU USE TO TOUCH?

You feel with every part of your body, from the top of your head to the tips of your toes. Your skin is covered with **receptors.** The receptors sense when you touch something.

You touch things with your hands and fingers, feet and toes. Your finger tips and the bottoms of your feet have the most receptors. The tip of your nose and the tip of your tongue are also **sensitive** to touch.

HOW DO YOU FEEL THINGS?

Your body is covered with skin. The skin has two **layers**. You can see the top layer. The next layer has **receptors**. They feel things that touch the skin.

The receptors sense hot and cold. They sense when a hair is moved. They sense when skin is pressed. **Nerves** take these messages to your brain. Your brain tells you that you have touched something.

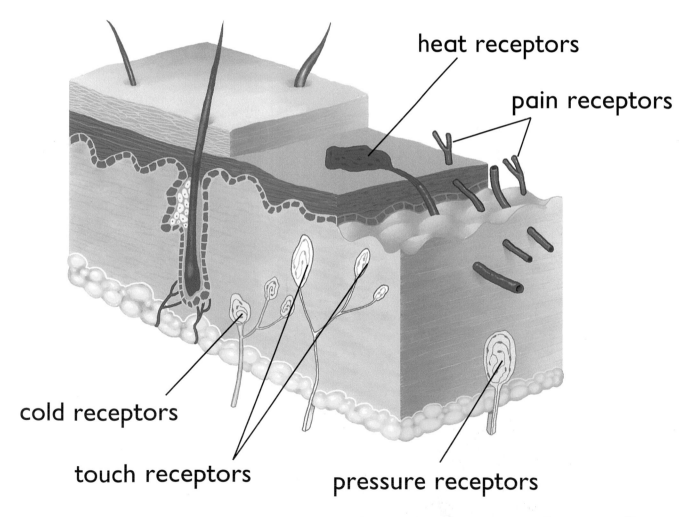

heat receptors

pain receptors

cold receptors

touch receptors

pressure receptors

USING TOUCH TO STAY SAFE

When you touch something, the message quickly goes to your brain. If it hurts, then your brain tells you to stop touching it.

People who are **blind** can use touch to tell them about things. A special writing called braille is read with the fingers. Braille is written with patterns of raised dots.

USING YOUR SENSE OF TOUCH

The **receptors** in your skin can feel if it is a hot day or a cold day. If it is hot, your body **perspires** to cool down. If it is cold, your body shivers to make you warmer.

Receptors tell you when someone presses hard or gently on your skin. Receptors tell you when someone tickles the palms of your hands and the bottoms of your feet.

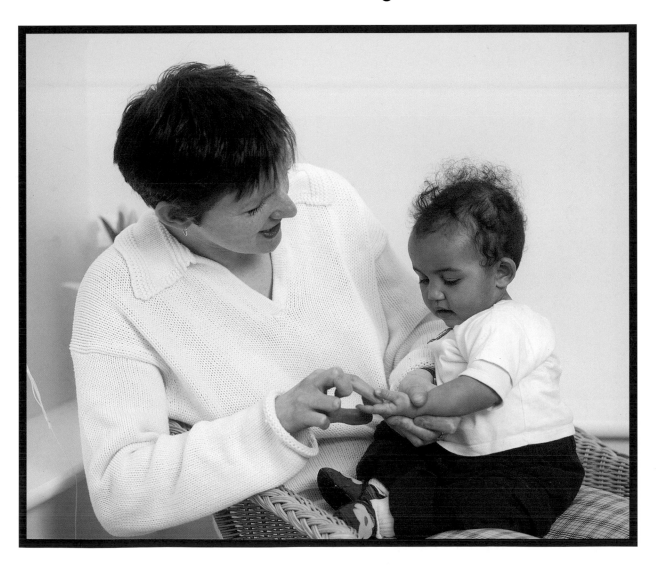

WHAT CAN HAPPEN TO TOUCH?

Sometimes hands cannot feel. They are **numb**. Illness or old age can make hands numb. This means that the **nerves** are not sending a message to the brain.

Cold weather can make your hands and feet feel numb. Sometimes you cannot pick up tiny things if your fingers are cold and numb.

ANIMALS AND TOUCH

Some animals use parts of their bodies like hands. A mother elephant gently strokes her calf with her trunk. A crocodile carefully carries her babies in her mouth.

A tiny baby kangaroo is born **blind.** It climbs up to its mother's **pouch** by feeling its way through her fur.

MORE ABOUT ANIMALS

A **sea anemone** waves **tentacles** in the water. When it feels food, it pushes the food into its mouth. Fish feel changes in the flow of water. This tells them when something is near.

Many animals use touch to **groom** each other. Monkeys stroke each other's fur to pick out **mites**. Some small fish clean bigger fish. They pick off **parasites** with their lips.

WHY DO PEOPLE TOUCH ANIMALS?

Veterinarians touch animals to help them. They rub their hands over the animal's body to feel for a broken bone. Their hands help them to find out why an animal has pain.

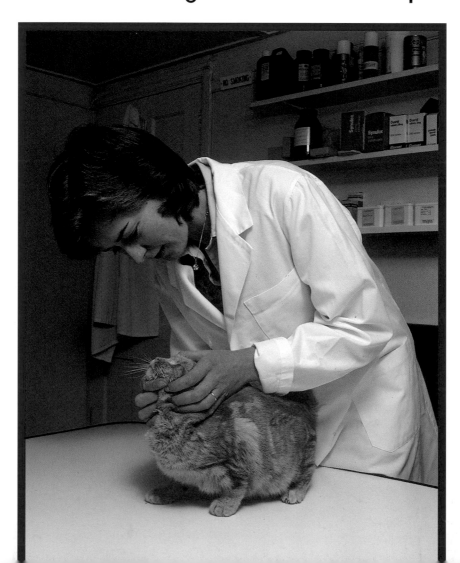

People like to stroke their pets. Cats and dogs rub themselves against people. They want to be stroked. A rider pats a horse to give it praise.

HOW DO ANIMALS KEEP SAFE?

A cat's whiskers help it feel the size of something. Whiskers tell a cat if it can get through a small space. If the whiskers can get through the space, so can the cat's body.

Water bugs spin around on top of
the water. They are careful not to bump
into each other. They put one of their
antennae on the water to feel **ripples**
made by other beetles.

INVESTIGATING TOUCH

Put on a pair of gloves. Can you feel the shape and size of things with your hands? Can you feel if things are warm or cold, sharp or prickly? Can you undo a button?

One girl wears gloves. The other does not. Do you think both girls can feel the stickiness of the dessert? Can both girls feel the hardness of the wood block?

Playing Tricks on Feeling

Some rides in amusement parks have soft, **wispy** things hanging down. They touch you as you go by. Your brain thinks they feel like spider webs. It's scary!

Put one hand in warm water. Put one hand in cold water. Then put both hands in **lukewarm** water. The water will feel hot to the cold hand and cold to the warm hand.

warm water

lukewarm water

cold water

DID YOU KNOW?

Some plants feed on small insects. The Venus flytrap has tiny hairs that feel a fly landing on it. When the hairs are moved, the plant snaps shut. It traps the fly inside.

If **receptors** in the skin feel cold, little hairs stand up on your skin. They do this to try to trap warm air. When the hairs stand up, they make bumps called goosebumps.

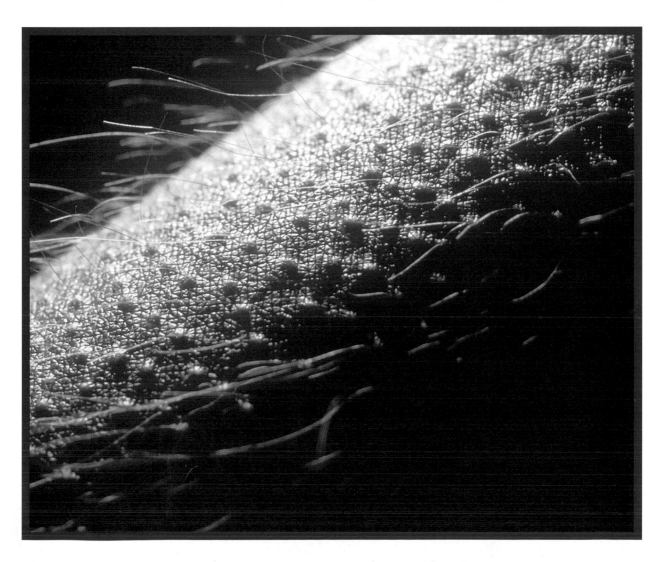

GLOSSARY

antenna (more than one are called antennae) long, thin growth that helps some animals to know what is around them.

blind not able to see

groom to brush the fur or skin to clean it

layer one covering of something

lukewarm not very warm or cold

mite very tiny insect

nerve something that carries messages from the body to the brain

numb not able to feel

parasite very tiny animal that lives on other animals

perspire to produce a salty liquid that cools the body, to sweat

pouch special pocket on a female kangaroo's body for carrying her babies

receptor cell in the body that can sense what is around it

ripple little wave on water

sea anemone animal that looks like a plant and lives on rocks in the sea (You say a-*nim*-muh-nee)

sensitive able to feel quickly

tentacle tube that sticks out from an animal's body

veterinarian doctor for animals

wispy strip of something very light and thin, such as string

SENSE MAP

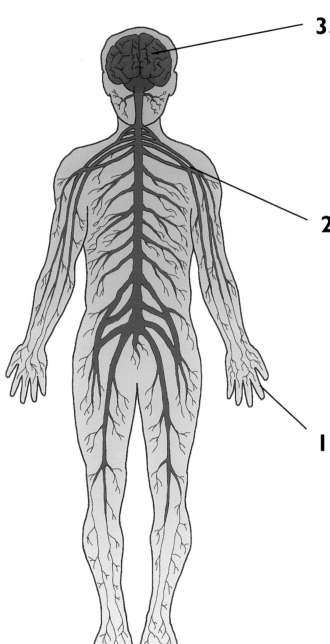

3. The brain recognizes touch messages.

2. Small nerves join up with bigger nerves and travel to the brain.

1. **Nerves** pick up messages from **receptors** in the skin. There are many receptors close together on the hands and feet.

31

MORE BOOKS TO READ

Hurwitz, Sue. *Touch*. New York: Rosen Publishing Group, 1997.

Pringle, Laurence. *Touch*. Tarrytown, N.Y.: Marshall Cavendish, 1999.

Walpole, Brenda. *Touch*. Austin, Tex.: Raintree Steck-Vaughn, 1996.

INDEX